The Power of Joy

The Power of Joy
A SUSTAINABLE SOURCE!

Dr. Cassandra McDonald

Copyright © 2017 Dr. Cassandra McDonald
All rights reserved.

Unless otherwise noted, all scripture references in this book are taken from the King James Version (KJV).

ISBN-13: 9780692871782
ISBN-10: 0692871780

Dr. Cassandra McDonald has been an inspiration to all those who know her or have been touched by her healing grace. Her belief in the Lord and our Almighty God permeates her lifetime as He called her to serve humanity, the poor, the downtrodden, and the hopeless with the Lord's message. Not only does she make visitations in local jails, but she also became an autism scholarship provider, through Ohio Department of Education, for our youth with autism. Blessed with the joy of music in her heart, her operatic voice soothes the savage beast within all of us as she sings and plays the piano. *The Power of Joy* represents a lifetime of faith. Joy of the Lord consumes Cassandra as it pours outward to heal, to love, to teach, and to believe. As a former public relations manager with a multinational corporation, nonprofits, and private companies and as a freelance writer for several years, all I can exclaim is, "Well worth reading to stimulate and to inspire your joy of the Lord."

—Cherie Lebrun

Dr. Cassandra McDonald has led a life of inspiration to all she has taught and served. In both the United States and in Latin America, her work in spreading the joy of music—singing, instrumental, and the creation of original songs—to students of many ages has uplifted and reenergized schools and communities. As an associate of foundations in the United States and abroad, Dr. McDonald's contributions have ennobled the vision to reach students who others considered unreachable. Kudos to Dr. McDonald. Her book is a must read!

—Doug Tedford, EdD
Author, *Identities* (Cengage Learning)
Owner, Teaching Services Latin America
Executive Education Committee, Rigoberta Menchu Foundation

Dr. Cassandra McDonald is a wonderful inspiration and gift to the community. Her words in this book speak life. They speak trust in God and His plan and His Word. The excerpts of Dr. McDonald's life make me realize that even when life gets uncontrollable, unbearable, and overwhelming, there is light and life at the end of the tunnel. I am forever changed and encouraged by her words. People need to read this book! It is as wonderful and amazing as Dr. McDonald is herself. I am forever grateful for her words.

—Keisha Pettijohn, MA, CDCA

Dr. Cassandra exudes joy in every moment, in every situation, day to day in her own life. Listening and letting the Lord work through her and guide her is always foremost in Dr. Cassandra McDonald's keys for living a happy, successful life. The same keys she used to raise her five beautiful children into leaders in their own careers and lives are what joyously lifted Dr. Cass to the heights of her own success and happiness. Now she is leading her readers to discover just how easily we each can live with an abundance of joy in our hearts.

—Lisa A. Olinger, BS, TB

As I reminisced about my first meeting with Dr. Cassandra, her presence filled the room. There was an undeniable light that overshadowed everything that was going on the inside the room as well as the storm that had invaded the darkness outside. Her light that she walked in pierced through all the distractions. The joy that was inside her has never stopped beaming, from that day up until now. I have learned it is easy to have joy when life is going good and when there is no darkness and no battles to fight. However, when my journey has been darted with pain, disappointments, and what may have seemed like the darkest hour, it was in those places that I would see this sustainable peace and joy shine though. Like all things, faith comes from hearing and hearing by the word of God. I am confident that as you read this book your midnight will come with the promise of that joy.

—Prophetess Toni M. Williams
Author, *It Was Something He Said*

Dedication

This book is dedicated to my five children, who are the loves of my life. They lived with me and through me, experiencing the God in me. They watched me process and grew along with me. They were part of the cause and purpose of my journey. They listened to and witnessed the miracles my God performed in me emotionally, physically, spiritually, and financially. As adults, they have dedicated their lives to God. They each have their own personal experiences of knowing what it means to choose God as first in their lives. We now communicate on such depth in His word and manifestation of joy in His Spirit.

Contents

Introduction · xi

Thought 1	Weight Lifter ·	1
Thought 2	Breaking Through The Darkness · · · · · · · · · · · · · · · · · · ·	5
Thought 3	God Growing Me ·	9
Thought 4	He Took My Load ·	13
Thought 5	Could Not Find Me ·	17
Thought 6	Just Let Him Fill You ·	21
Thought 7	Fruit Tree on a Null Hill · · · · · · · · · · · · · · · · · · ·	25
Thought 8	Be Fruity ·	29
Thought 9	Overwhelming Joy ·	33
Thought 10	Bursting ·	37
Thought 11	Covered ·	41
Thought 12	Be Strategic ·	45
Thought 13	Value Yourself ·	49
Thought 14	What If I Squeeze? ·	53
Thought 15	Guarded ·	57
Thought 16	Fast-Forward ·	61
Thought 17	New Growth ·	65
Thought 18	From Down Under ·	69
Thought 19	Learning to Grow ·	73
Thought 20	Listening ·	77
Thought 21	Complete ·	81

Thought 22	God Is All in All	85
Thought 23	God's Promise	89
Thought 24	Three Become One	93
Thought 25	Releasing	97
Thought 26	Balance	101
Thought 27	Tranquility!	105
Thought 28	Waiting through Winter	109
Thought 29	Perfect Peace	113
Thought 30	Complete Joy	117

Introduction

▲ ▲ ▲

THIS IS A JOURNEY OF my thoughts as I was inspired by God to share with you. It all started when I became a freshman at college. I had just received God's Holy Spirit into my life three days before leaving for college. Although I had been raised in church and knew how to live as someone who is saved, I embarked on a journey that enabled me to find Jesus for myself. I discovered that His joy is a sustainable source.

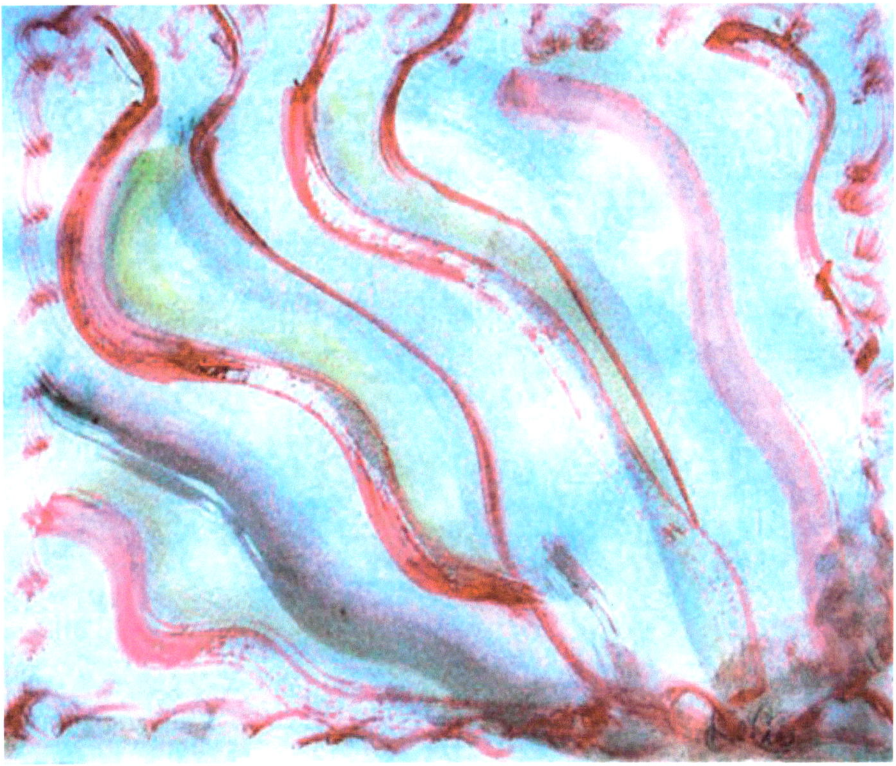

THOUGHT 1

Weight Lifter

> **My brethren, count it all joy when ye fall into divers temptations; Knowing *this,* that the trying of your faith worketh patience. But let patience have *her* perfect work, that ye may be perfect and entire, wanting nothing. If any of you lack wisdom, let him ask of God, that giveth to all *men* liberally, and upbraideth not; and it shall be given him. (James 1:2–6)**

WHAT DOES THIS SCRIPTURE MEAN? I recall a time when I had just left home for college. The pressures and stresses of college had begun to blur my vision of happiness. I found myself in a situation where I was trying to please my parents and the newfound love of my life by earning a 4.0. I was so miserable. As I was walking along one day after it had rained, I saw a puddle of water. I said to myself, "Oh, I wish I had the nerve to put my nose into those three inches of water and just disappear." My stresses weighed me down at the time. That night I had a dream. In the dream the scripture James 105 came to me. I was confused because that combination of numbers does not exist in the book of James in the Holy Bible. I finally figured it out—it meant James 1:5. God was telling me that I had to wait with patience and with joy. God has given me this same scripture for the last forty years, and it still works. I have a much better understanding of it now. He has lifted my weights!

Your Thoughts

THOUGHT 2

Breaking Through The Darkness

> **Therefore being justified by faith, we have peace with God through our Lord Jesus Christ: By whom also we have access by faith into this grace wherein we stand, and rejoice in hope of the glory of God. And not only *so,* but we glory in tribulations also: knowing that tribulations worketh patience; And patience, experience; and experience, hope: And hope maketh not ashamed; because the love of God is shed abroad in our hearts by the Holy Ghost which is given unto us. (Romans 5:1–5)**

WHAT A PRIVILEGE TO SERVE God and to be trusted with the challenge of obeying Him. God trusted me to represent Him through my faith in Him. As a new babe in Christ, I decided to choose God, even if it meant being set apart from the crowd. Daniel and the Hebrew boys passed the tests they were given. Their faith was challenged to trust God as their only true source. They trusted God as a lover of their souls. When their lives depended on it, they depended on God. I had to break through my dark thoughts and into God's thoughts. His ways and thoughts are so much higher than my logical thought patterns. He is a faithful God. I must learn to believe what I cannot see. I have hope when I look through God's eyes.

Your Thoughts

THOUGHT 3

GOD GROWING ME

▲▲▲

> **And when they saw him, they worshipped him: but some doubted. And Jesus came and spake unto them, saying; All power is given unto me in heaven and in earth. (Matthew 28:18)**

ONE NIGHT, ALL NIGHT LONG, God said to me, "To the power of, to the power of!" The next day He told me, "I am the power of! Use my math. It is always to the power of—more abundantly above all that you can ask or think!"

> **Now unto him that is able to do exceeding abundantly above all that we ask or think, according to the power that worketh in us. (Ephesians 3:20)**

THE POWER OF ONE
ONE =1,000
TWO=10,000
THREE=100,000
FOUR=1,000,000
FIVE=10,000,000

This is how God multiplies. He deals with me using the number five, which represents grace and favor. God told me, "Get excited about learning more about Me. Study Me and My Word. Seek and desire to grow in Me!"

Your Thoughts

THOUGHT 4

HE TOOK MY LOAD

For God so loved the world, that he gave his only begotten Son, that whosoever believeth in him should not perish, but have everlasting life. (John 3:16)

IF ONLY WE COULD EMBRACE and understand the love that God has for us. The love God has for us is enough love to carry us through any situation. If His promises are true—and they are—then He promises no more than we can bear and that with a way of escape (I Corinthians 10:13). God has taken unbearable pain away from me in an instant. He has carried my loads. He is the author and finisher of our faith. Who, for the joy, before Him endured the cross barring the pain of sin. Jesus died so that we do not have to die in sin!

At thirty-eight, I thought to myself, "Is this all there is going to be in life?" I had birthed my fifth child, and I wanted more from life than birthing babies. Why was I given these gifts and talents? I would wake up each morning asking God, "What were you thinking?" I was depressed and did not know it. I asked my mentor if anything was going to happen in my life before I turned forty. She told me that God can do a lot in two years.

One day Marvelous Marvin, a renowned motivational speaker, was on the front page of the newspaper. He was to speak at Muskingum University for Black History Month. I said aloud, "Lord, I should be singing at this event." To my surprise, I received a phone call and was invited to lead the worship service before this speaker.

Dr. Beaver, Muskingum College's chaplain, said to me, "I want some fire in this Presbyterian church service!" Before I was forty, I was singing with the symphony, including one of my original compositions! Nothing but God's love for me caused these events to occur. Waiting on God's perfect timing is worth it. I had birthed five babies, and now it was my time!

Your Thoughts

THOUGHT 5

COULD NOT FIND ME

Come unto me, all ye that labour and are heavy laden, and I will give you rest. Take my yoke upon you, and learn of me; for I am meek and lowly in heart: and ye shall find rest unto your souls. For my yoke is easy, and my burden is light. (Matthew 11:28)

WHEN I HAD NO IDEA how I was going to bear the next moment, God would say, "You don't have to. I'll bear it for you." This is how good my God is to me. How good do you allow your God to be to you? He will do the same for you just like He did for me. What is my singleness of purpose? What are my words of uniqueness that God created to bring me to my message and my world-changing assignment? I choose to believe God beyond my visible capabilities. God sang this song in my ear, and it saved me! "I Have a Purpose for You in Your Life!" Every time I had a dark thought I sang this song. It cleared me to find myself, allowing me to fulfill my purpose. (Included on CD is "Just Let Him.")

Your Thoughts

THOUGHT 6

JUST LET HIM FILL YOU

> **Jesus answered and said unto her, If thou knewest the gift of God, and who it is that saith to thee, Give me to drink; thou wouldest have asked of him, and he would have given thee living water. Whosoever drinketh of this water shall thirst again: But whosoever drinketh of the water that I shall give him shall never thirst; but the water that I shall give him shall be in him a well of water springing up into everlasting life. (John 4:10–14)**

FILL MY CUP, LORD. WHEN Jesus told the woman at the well who she was, her life became purposeful. She had tried to find herself through her many husbands, but that was not her identity. When Jesus filled her cup, He gave her self-value and self-worth. He told her who she really was. He revealed her self-truth in life. No longer was she ashamed. She had something significant to talk and shout about. She proclaimed who her Lord and Savior was!

Once I became as one in Christ, I knew I was chosen to be a global ambassador for Him! The purpose of my life was to represent Christ on earth. Just as He did the work of His Father, I was chosen to follow Him and be just like Him. Amazing fulfillment! When I look in the mirror, Jesus should see Himself!

Your Thoughts

THOUGHT 7

FRUIT TREE ON A NULL HILL

The joy of the Lord is my strength. (Nehemiah 8:10)

**Rejoice in the Lord always and again I
say rejoice! (Philippians 4:4)**

**But the fruit of the Spirit is love, joy, peace, longsuffering,
gentleness, goodness, faith, Meekness, temperance:
against such there is no law. (Galatians 5:22)**

ALL THE FRUITS OF THE Spirit are mine if I plan to exercise them. How can I be kind to someone today? How can I show love today? This fruit of love and kindness will bring me fruit of love and kindness. As you become an advocate of the fruit, the fruit becomes your attribute! If your purpose is to promote the fruit of the Spirit, then you will possess the fruit of the Spirit. The fruitier you are, the fruitier you will be! The more fruit you give, the more fruit you will receive. Strive to be a fruit-giving tree!

The Power of Joy

Your Thoughts

THOUGHT 8

BE FRUITY

> **O give thanks unto the LORD; for *he is* good: for his mercy *endureth* for ever. (Psalm 136:1)**

If I work the fruit of the Spirit (Galatians 5:22–23), the fruit of the Spirit will also work for me. The key is to be thankful: fruit begets fruit. If the fruit of the Spirit is not producing, God says to cut the tree down. He expects us to be fruity. He expects us to exhibit the attributes of the fruit. We need to examine ourselves and see if we are increasing in love, joy, peace, and all the fruit of the spirit. God expects us to represent Him. When situations come up, we are supposed to respond like we are children of God. When there is a non-peaceful situation, think peace, seek peace, and the God of peace will send peace! In every situation, be fruity representing God. He will show up and change situations, being the great God that He is. He said, "I come that you might have life and that more abundantly" (John 10:10), so we are to speak life into whatever situation is present. He is the giver of life, and we are His handiwork; that is why He put His Holy Spirit in us. We have power over every situation!

Your Thoughts

THOUGHT 9

OVERWHELMING JOY

And we know that all things work together for good to them that love God, to them who are the called according to His purpose. (Romans 8:28)

IN ALL THINGS GIVE THANKS because giving thanks brings joy! If I am thankful about a situation, then I am not bitter about it. I can trust God and believe that He knows what He is doing and that He will work it out for my good. "And we know that all things work together for good to them that love God, to them who are the called according to His purpose" (Romans 8:28). Trusting in God and having the confidence to wait for what He is doing is vital! He is the only one who lives in the future. Being overwhelmed with joy comes through knowing that God knows what is good for us.

Your Thoughts

THOUGHT 10

Bursting

> **Rejoice in the Lord always; and again I say, rejoice. (Philippians 4:4)**

> **Thou wilt keep him in perfect peace, whose mind is stayed on thee: because he trusteth in thee. (Isaiah 26:3)**

IF WE TAKE CARE OF God's business, He will take care of ours. Keeping your mind focused on Him will give you a peace that passes all understanding. No pity parties. Do not focus on yourself, but focus on the Author and Finisher of your faith, Jesus! Father knows best! He created us in His image and finds pleasure when we prosper. His intent is to bless us according to his riches in glory. I say to my Father often, "You are rich. I am your child, so that makes me rich too!" Knowing that you are rich and do not need anything because your Father has promised to supply it is very peaceful. Just believe!

Your Thoughts

THOUGHT 11

COVERED

> **Finally, my brethren, be strong in the Lord, and in the power of his might. Put on the whole armour of God, that ye may be able to stand against the wiles of the devil. For we wrestle not against flesh and blood, but against principalities, against powers, against the rulers of the darkness of this world, against spiritual wickedness in high places. Wherefore take unto you the whole armour of God, that ye may be able to withstand in the evil day, and having done all, to stand. Stand therefore, having your loins girt about with truth, and having on the breastplate of righteousness. (Ephesians 6:10)**

ARMOR UP! WHERE IS YOUR ammunition? Do not get caught with your guard down. Put on the whole armor of God (Ephesians 6:11). Our God covers our multitude of sins with His love. Whatever we are confronted with, we know Jesus has already conquered it. We can trust that he will keep us and protect us, even through pain. Sometimes God removes our pain immediately. Other times, He builds our tenacity and endurance while we are going through pain. Nevertheless, we know the outcome is that we will win. This increases our conquering of fearless faith. There is a war going on. God said you will have tribulation, but be of good cheer. I have overcome the world (John 16:33)! Remember that we are always protected.

Your Thoughts

THOUGHT 12

BE STRATEGIC

> **If ye keep my commandments, ye shall abide in my love; even as I have kept my Father's commandments, and abide in his love. These things have I spoken unto you, that my joy might remain in you, and that your joy might be full. (John 15:10–11)**

PLAN TO HAVE JOY. PLAN ahead. Rehearse positive responses to stimulated situations. Plan not to respond out of anger, but wait on the Lord. Pray first! Be strategic like the military trains its army. Train yourself to wait. Be disciplined. Allow the joy of the Lord to be your strength and not your anger. Your response must be spiritual and not emotional. God says that your joy may be full. Exercise your right to be joyous! Jesus said, "I came that you might have life and that more abundantly" (John 10:10). The joy of the Lord is my strength (Nehemiah 8:10). Through His strength, receive love and joy. That is the way God gives it!

Your Thoughts

THOUGHT 13

VALUE YOURSELF

**I am the true vine, and my Father is the husbandman.
Every branch in me that beareth not fruit he taketh away:
and every *branch* that beareth fruit, he purgeth it, that
it may bring forth more fruit. Now ye are clean through
the word which I have spoken unto you. (John 15:1)**

YOU HAVE GOT TO BE hooked up. Do not cut yourself off from the vine and act like you are not your Father's child. God guarantees that He will bless you abundantly, above all than you can ask or think, if you will abide in Him and His Word abides in you. This is a God who wants us to live without struggle. God is very strategic in how He keeps His children who will stay connected with Him. When I was going through some of my deepest tests that I could not pull myself out of, God would bring along somebody who had a desperate need, and I would have to encourage them and help them. In the midst of doing that, I would forget about my problems, and the end result was that I was encouraged. These distractions can help you when you are weak. "Let the weak say I am strong" (Joel 3:10). In our weakness, we can be strong in Him. It is so important to keep your communication of praise and worship daily. I have a saying: "Praise is the perfect place of peace!" When you worship in the spirit, you do not feel pain, stress, or broken bones. You are taken away with the Lord. Where God is, those things do not exist. So keep your connection, even though the adversary will bring strong delusions. Praise God! Value yourself like God values you. Keep your vine alive!

Your Thoughts

THOUGHT 14

WHAT IF I SQUEEZE?

For as he thinketh in his heart, so is he. (Proverbs 23:7)

The Angel of the Lord appeared unto him and said unto him, The Lord is with thee, thou mighty man of valor. And the Lord said unto him, Surely I will be with thee, and thou shalt smite the Midianites as one man. (Judges 6:12, 16)

WHAT ARE YOU FULL OF? Be careful what you feed your spirit. Build your faith from the inside out. What is in your stuffing? If I take a bite of your stuffing or squeeze, what will come out? The apple looks good on the outside, but what is in its core? A worm? You are who God says you are! Oftentimes we do not know what is in us. Generally, we have been told who and what we are. That is not how God intended for us to be. Gideon replied to the angel by describing himself as left-handed, poor, and the least in his father's house. I had to learn how to listen to the voice of God. He told me the great things He had planned for my life. It took me a while to learn not to share God's promises for me with everyone. God demanded intimacy in our relationship. He wanted me to trust Him and not validate His word with another human being. Trust and obey like Gideon, and watch what God does in your life!

Your Thoughts

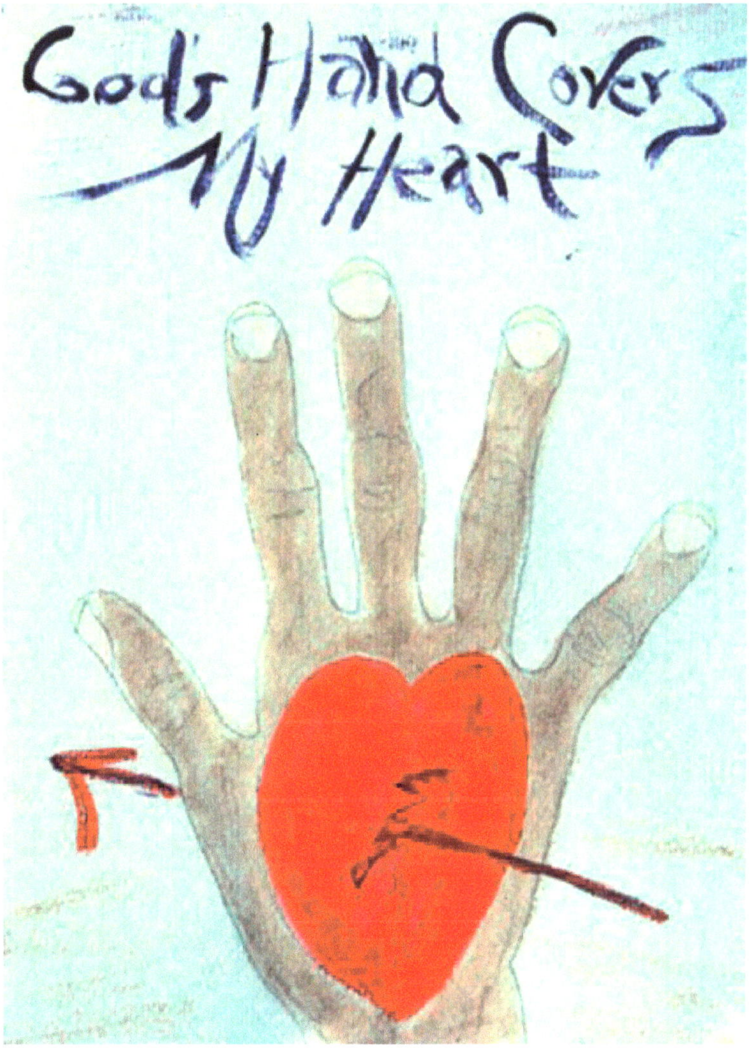

THOUGHT 15

GUARDED

Therefore if any man be in Christ, he is a new creature: old things are passed away; behold, all things are become new. (II Corinthians 5:17)

THE MILITARY SIMULATES WARFARE SITUATIONS and drills so that the troops can prepare themselves. This prepares them for battle! They learn how to respond and how not to react when confronted with various situations. We need to prepare in much the same way. We need to condition our minds and hearts to respond in a godly manner.

Our responses have to line up with the word of God. God has to be the captain of the army. He has to be the one who is giving the orders. We follow His lead, and He will guide our every footstep. He will not let our feet slip. God knows our every thought before we think them. If we give Him charge over our lives, He will guard us. He says He knows the thoughts He has for us, and they are not of evil. He rejoices when we prosper.

Your Thoughts

THOUGHT 16

Fast-Forward

> **Before I formed thee in the belly I knew thee; and before thou camest forth out of the womb I sanctified thee, *and* I ordained thee a prophet unto the nations. (Jeremiah 1:5)**

How do I get my joy to stay? By doing the will of the Lord. Since the beginning of time, God had a perfect purpose designed for us. Choose to stay under the shadow of His wings. He will fast-forward you to safety and maintain your joy. God inhabits praise. So go where He lives to keep your joy. For His joy is your strength—use Him. He is your Father. I can always come to my Father. He always receives me with open arms. He is my safe place. My Father provides a shield and a buckler from the fiery darts of the enemy. I have found the reason why the song "Jesus Loves Me" is my favorite song. He loves me like no one else can or will. His love is a constant. My father's love provides stability, longevity, and favor!

Your Thoughts

THOUGHT 17

NEW GROWTH

A little leaven leavens the whole loaf. (I Corinthians 5:6)

BEING PURE FROM THE ROOT gives you the ability to have new growth when you need it. Geraniums, for example, must be pruned continually—you must pop off the old to make room for new growth. I once put a pot of geraniums on my porch, and every time I went into my house, I plucked off the dead ends so that the whole plant did not die, thus enabling new growth. If anything clogs your joy, pop it off. It has to go. Do not give anybody or anything that much power or control in your life. It has to go. Pop off anyone or anything that interferes with your joy so you can grow. If you do not, it will kill you. Geraniums have to breathe, so popping off the dead part of the stem will give it new breath. A little leaven leavens the whole loaf (I Corinthians 5:6). Just like your answering machine will only hold so many messages before you have to delete some messages to make room for more, God wants you to be focused on spiritual growth. So pop off the dead stems and make room for new growth.

Your Thoughts

THOUGHT 18

FROM DOWN UNDER

And that which fell among thorns are they, which, when they have heard, go forth, and are choked with cares and riches and pleasures of *this* life, and bring no fruit to perfection. But that on the good ground are they, which in an honest and good heart, having heard the word, keep *it*, and bring forth fruit with patience. (Luke 8:15)

WE CAME FROM DIRT JUST like the seed-bearing food that we eat. Now we produce seed to seed. There is something about that dirt—we still need nurturing from it. God can move on fallow ground. He is willing to sow into good ground that is willing to be cultivated. Which will it be, His will or my will? Lord, I am willing push through my dirt, from down under, to new life.

Your Thoughts

THOUGHT 19

LEARNING TO GROW

> **Even so the tongue is a little member, and boasteth great things. Behold, how great a matter a little fire kindleth! And the tongue is a fire, a world of iniquity: so is the tongue among our members, that it defileth the whole body, and setteth on fire the course of nature; and it is set on fire of hell. Therewith bless we God, even the Father; and therewith curse we men, which are made after the similitude of God. Out of the same mouth proceedeth blessing and cursing. But the wisdom that is from above is first pure, then peaceable, gentle, and easy to be intreated, full of mercy and good fruits, without partiality, and without hypocrisy. And the fruit of righteousness is sown in peace of them that make peace. (James 3:5–17)**

READ THE BOOK OF JAMES. It is amazing how much words hurt. I remember thinking, "I did not just fail this test—I flunked it miserably!" I was caught with my guard down. I must guard my heart carefully. I did not put God first. I said exactly what was on my mind, not what should have been in my heart. It is most difficult and at best impossible to erase words that hurt. My commitment and assignment is to be the one who helps and doesn't hurt people. I must immediately forgive and not respond out of my hurt. My connection with God is strong enough to heal my all hurts. Based on my actions, the fruit of the Spirit was not present. I knew this, but I had not learned how to grow my faith in this area. I need to grow stronger in the Word, doubling up on my faith-strengthening exercises. Be a peacemaker!

Your Thoughts

THOUGHT 20

LISTENING

> **And so he that had received five talents came and brought other five talents, saying, Lord, thou deliveredst unto me five talents: behold, I have gained beside them five talents more. His lord said unto him, Well done, *thou* good and faithful servant: thou hast been faithful over a few things, I will make thee ruler over many things: enter thou into the joy of thy lord. (Matthew 25:20–21)**

I CAN ONLY HEAR GOD when I am listening. If I am full of myself at any given moment, then I am not full of Him and have become a cog in the wheel. We should continually strive to let God be Lord in our lives. The first year I had my music camp, I learned a very important lesson. God gave me the phrase, "When you release fear, you can hear." As long as I am in my thoughts, I cannot hear the directions of the Lord. Once I trust him fully, realizing I have absolutely no control anyway, then I can hear his voice ever so clear. He allowed me to learn that. He is my only source, and He is the one who provides resources. It is not my thoughts and my efforts that provide but God's! That same year, God directed me to go to a restaurant. My intent was to ask for giveaways for my music camp. The manager was a person I had not seen for years. He asked me how he could help me as he had the next two weeks off. He knew absolutely nothing about my situation. God had planted it in his heart to say this to me. He was a gourmet chef! He kicked off my camp with an incredible blessing! That was fourteen years ago. C.A.S.S. (Creating Artist Stimulating Success) Camp is a business, art, and music (BAM) camp for kindergarten through twelfth grade. God is good!

Your Thoughts

THOUGHT 21

Complete

> **Trust in the lord with all of thine heart. And lean not unto thing own understanding. In all of thy ways acknowledge him. And he will direct your path. (Proverbs 3: 56)**

God, do I love you enough? Are you the first and only one, the only power and source in my life? Are you the controlling source? Do I give you total control so that I hand over my doubts and fears to Your hand for You to do as You will? Do I say yes to your will, realizing that you are in total control? Do I trust You and Your judgment without question, even though it hurts so bad I really want to do something to eliminate the pain so I can be happy? Real happiness and joy only come from You. How can I obtain it? What is it?

God came to me and asked me, "If I tell you to go, and if I tell you where and when will you go?"

After asking myself what would these five people in my life say, I replied to God, "Oh Lord, you're not first!" I am not like Abraham, who was told to go and did not know where he was going and said, "Yes, Lord." I realized I still have a lot of work to do. I asked God to forgive me. I want to be complete in Him.

YOUR THOUGHTS

THOUGHT 22

GOD IS ALL IN ALL

▲▲▲

> **The LORD *is* my light and my salvation; whom shall I fear? the LORD *is* the strength of my life; of whom shall I be afraid?…*I had fainted,* unless I had believed to see the goodness of the LORD in the land of the living. Wait on the LORD: be of good courage, and he shall strengthen thine heart: wait, I say, on the LORD. (Psalm 27: 1,13–14)**

When I am tempted, drawn away by my own lust to satisfy my anger, hurt, or to do it my way, to satisfy my own will *now*, do I love God enough to wait for Him? Do I love and trust Him enough to wait for Him to help me solve my problems? Can and will I humble my will to God's will? Will I be of good courage and keep my joy? Is He my all in all? The Lord came to me again five years later with the same question, minus one detail: "If I tell you to go, and I tell you where, will you go?"

My response was, "Lord, I am better, but I am still serving fear!"

A few years later in 2011, I went to Guatemala after being invited to the Pavarotti School of Art. I took a team of business, art, and music professionals with me. Wow! Through the miraculous works of God's presence, I was freed from my fears. I told God, "You do not have to ask me again. I am on Go! I am ready to go wherever, however, and whenever You tell me to go!" It feels so good to live free in God—free from the influences of people, places, and things other than God, who is the source of my full joy!

Your Thoughts

THOUGHT 23

God's Promise

▲▲▲

May the God of hope fill you with all joy and peace in believing, so that by the power of the Holy Spirit you may abound in hope. (Romans 15:13)

And he said, The things which are impossible with men are possible with God. (Luke 18:27)

IF YOU ARE NOT FEELING joy in your life, then take a look at yourself and not someone else. You are the only one who can change you. Take an introspective look and decide what changes you need to make to be happy and to experience the joy God promised you. That promise of joy can be powerful. Grab on to it because the joy of the Lord is your strength. I had a person within my personal inner circle tell me I was nothing. I asked to repeat that! Then he used the scriptures to try to clean that statement up. Unfortunately, most of us have experienced hurt like that in our lives. I knew it was not true, but it still hurt. God is such a comforter. He said to go home and write down everything I have accomplished. I could not count the number of souls I had helped receive the baptism of the water and Spirit—there were countless numbers. I wrote down the different organizations I had created, impacting lives. Not to pat myself on the back, but to know how God has strengthened me to be effective is amazing. God wanted to give me courage to become a world changer! Because I listened to His voice only, fruit was produced! We often measure ourselves by other people, but God's measurements are the fruit of His spirit working in our lives. It is a great thing to depend on God to do the impossible. That is exactly what His joy does! Oh, how I love Thee!

Your Thoughts

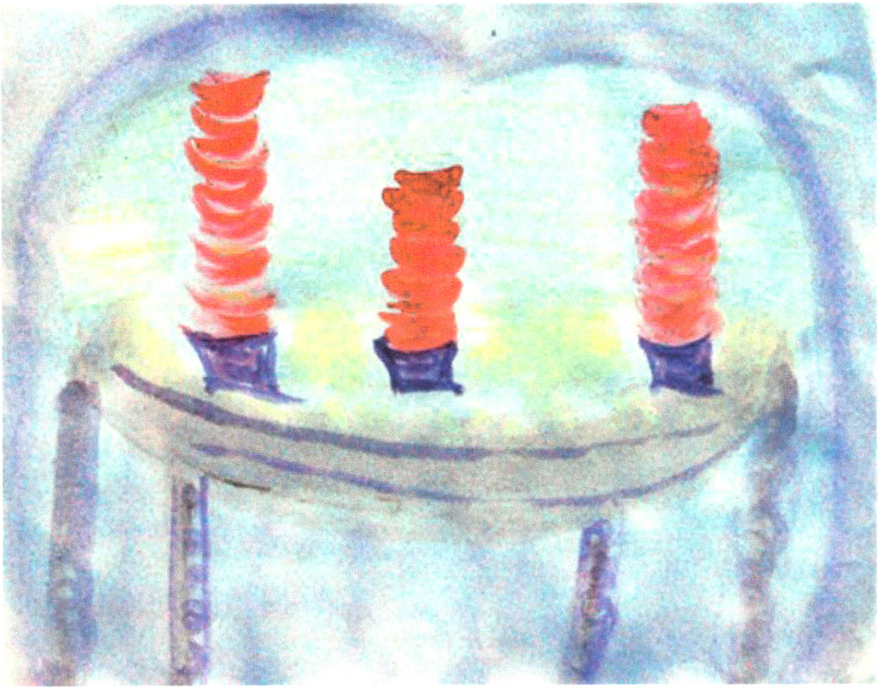

THOUGHT 24

Three Become One

> **Finally, my brethren, be strong in the Lord, and
> in the power of his might. (Ephesians 6:10)**

> **Thou shalt not be afraid for the terror by night; nor for the
> arrow that flieth by day; Nor for the pestilence that walketh
> in darkness; nor for the destruction that wasteth at noonday.
> A thousand shall fall at thy side, and ten thousand at thy
> right hand; but it shall not come nigh thee. (Psalm 91:6–8)**

How do you become strong and powerful in the Lord? God cannot use you when you are full of yourself. You have to be full of Him by killing your flesh all day, every day! Stay humble and respond to people and situations in a godly manner. When Joshua was left with the task of leading the Hebrew children into the Promised Land after Moses died, God commanded him to be of good courage. God told him there would not be any man who would be able to stand before him all the days of his life. As with Moses, God will not fail thee or forsake thee (Joshua 1:5). God let Joshua know that the Promised Land was his, but he would to have to fight for it.

I often heard the voice of the Lord saying to me, "There is a war going on—choose your weapons carefully!"

I always have the same response: "Lord, I really do not want to fight. I want to be a person of peace. I will wait for you to fix it!" That went on for years. Finally, I was in a position where I had no choice but to fight. I had to become strong in Him. The Lord equipped me for battle. Oh my, what a battle! God sent messages through visions and dreams to strengthen me. When you combine your mind, soul, and body to become as one, standing on God's promises without wavering or doubting, you win. He will allow all of your enemies to see you win! Greater is He that is in me than he that is in the world!

Your Thoughts

THOUGHT 25

RELEASING

> **Thou wilt keep him in perfect peace, whose mind is stayed on thee: because he trusteth in thee. Trust ye in the Lord for ever: for in the Lord Jehovah is everlasting strength. (Isaiah 26:3–4)**
>
> **And the peace of God, which passeth all understanding, shall keep your hearts and minds through Christ Jesus. (Philippians 4:7)**

I DID NOT RESPOND OUT of my hurt or anger, once again, before a vocal performance. Because I chose not to release my emotions verbally, it brought me to tears. It was the only release defense that was safe. I did not want to cry, nor did I want to respond in anger, which I knew would backfire. It was just like adding water to a fire—a way of containing the situation, remaining silent. Even though I could not keep the hurt inside, I was able to release the pain enough so that I could sleep in peace. I was thankful that God had given me enough strength to endure, to take the pain. Where is the joy in this? What do I say to myself to make myself joyful? The joy is in knowing that my Father who loves me has kept and protected me through this. The joy is in knowing I have produced growth within myself. I have allowed God to handle my situation. The results were that God anointed my performance as guest vocal soloist, accompanied by a one-hundred bell choir. It was excellent. He is a stabilizer! We always have choices. One choice is to rest in Him and let Him fight your battle, and another choice is to fight while He watches. When you choose to allow God to fight for you, there is a peace that comes, passing all understanding!

Your Thoughts

THOUGHT 26

BALANCE

The Lord is my shepherd; I shall not want. He maketh me to lie down in green pastures: he leadeth me beside the still waters. He restoreth my soul: he leadeth me in the paths of righteousness for his name's sake. Yea, though I walk through the valley of the shadow of death, I will fear no evil: for thou art with me; thy rod and thy staff they comfort me. Thou preparest a table before me in the presence of mine enemies: thou anointest my head with oil; my cup runneth over. Surely goodness and mercy shall follow me all the days of my life: and I will dwell in the house of the Lord for ever. (Psalm 23)

GOD IS A GOD OF compassion. He is in the midst, handling your situation. He hears and feels your hurt, and during your painful periods you can rejoice in Him because He makes the difference. His love makes me feel good. I love the way He loves me. God is the Equalizer. God takes the giants in your life and equalizes the battle ground so that your enemies are at your feet. You become the victor! Because God is the only one who lives in the future, He has already been there and done that. He knows precisely what it is going to take to win. For Him there are no surprises. Because He never loses, I have the great advantage.

I had a meeting where everyone was 100 percent against what I was there for. But I made my mind up before I went into the meeting that I would walk out a winner, and while I was there I was going to have fun. So when I needed a yes from everyone and everyone said no, I said, "Well, God, let me just sit back and watch you work. They all talked themselves into saying yes, and I walked out with the favor of God on my side. He will balance your whole life with His love if you let Him.

Your Thoughts

THOUGHT 27

Tranquility!

> **And Jabez was more honorable than his brethren: and his mother called his name Jabez, saying, Because I bare him with sorrow. And Jabez called on the God of Israel, saying, Oh that thou wouldest bless me indeed, and enlarge my coast, and that thine hand might be with me, and that thou wouldest keep me from evil, that it may not grieve me! And God granted him that which he requested. (I Chronicles 4:9–10)**

GOD'S PEACE WILL GIVE YOU joy. He knows the end before the beginning, so trusting and never doubting Him will give you peace. He is a win-win God. He will always win, so stick with the winner—Jesus. Stay on the team that always wins the gold medal. Gold medalists prepare for years. We only have to prepare our hearts each day so God can release it. That is one of my quotes. You have to speak favor into and over your life. Say what it is you believe; it increases your faith. God moves for you because of your faith. Jesus did not let even His own mother frame His future. His requests from God was that He do His will. God honored that. Remember, life and death is in the power of your tongue. You create your world by your words. So as a man thinketh, so is he. Watch your words! Speak peace and tranquility over your very being!

The Power of Joy

Your Thoughts

THOUGHT 28

Waiting through Winter

> **But they that wait upon the LORD shall renew *their* strength; they shall mount up with wings as eagles; they shall run, and not be weary; *and* they shall walk, and not faint. (Isaiah 40:31)**

> **But if we hope for that we see, then do we with patients wait for it. And we know that all things work together for good to them that love God, to them who are the called according to his purpose. (Romans 8:25, 28)**

Give thanks now. Keep your joy. You will have something to be thankful for, so you may as well give thanks now. In everything give thanks. We know that God is working it out for our good. When I waited on the Lord for a physical healing, I told God, "This is my body that I have dedicated to you. Either heal me or kill me." I believed that I was not finished with my purpose and that God would heal me—and he did. Even though medically I should have died that night, I did not.

I know God will cover you during your period of waiting. His love covers a multitude of sins. Fear creates sin, but perfect love casts out sin because God is love. It is not a risk to trust in God. It is a risk *not* to trust God. God said, "Beloved, I wish above all things that you prosper, be in good health as your soul prospers" (Romans 8:37). The key factor is to keep your soul lined up in the perfect will of God in His purpose. By seeking Him first, all these other things will be added unto you (Matthew 6:33). God is a keeper of His promises. Wait for more abundance than you can ever ask or imagine. God's word is *truth*!

Your Thoughts

THOUGHT 29

PERFECT PEACE

> **Be ye angry, and sin not: let not the sun go down upon your wrath. Let no corrupt communication proceed out of your mouth. (Ephesians 4:26, 29)**

THE QUALITY OF YOUR ABILITY to wait determines the quality of your joy. Let patience have her perfect work. Praise is the perfect place of peace! Delay is the best antidote to anger and being anxious. I want to pass my stress test with God, although I sometimes want to be angry and tell someone off just because it feels good. But does serving God feel better?

Exercising patience gives me peace. I have experienced 100 percent of the time that if I speak out of my frustration and anger, I am always wrong. I do not have clarity of thinking. My emotions are running high. My stress level and my blood pressure are up. Whatever I choose to say will not be laced with God's goodness. If I use the antidote of delaying my response, the outcome is much more positive. This antidote applies even when I have lost something and am intensely looking for it, having raised emotions, and I cannot find it. The item can be sitting right there in front of me. My vision and my thinking are blurred. I cannot find it. But when I truly give thanks and begin to worship, praising the Lord, I distract myself from my concerns. Then I can hear from God, and He speaks to me and tells me exactly what I need to know. Praise is the perfect place of peace! It works every time!

The Power of Joy

Your Thoughts

THOUGHT 30

COMPLETE JOY

> **Hitherto have ye asked nothing in my name: ask, and ye shall receive, that your joy may be full. (John 16:24)**
>
> **Whom having not seen, ye love; in whom, though now ye see him not, yet believing, ye rejoice with joy unspeakable and full of glory: Receiving the end of your faith, even the salvation of your souls. (I Peter 1:8–9)**

How to keep your joy:

> Humble yourself and lean not to your own understanding.
> Believe God without wavering.
> Trust God with your whole heart.
> Put your heart in His hands.
> Allow God to guard your heart.
> Refrain from testing God to see if He is real.

God, will You really do this? Can I trust You? Just put it in His hands and leave it there, knowing whatever He does will be perfect. Like Daniel and the Hebrew boys, it is your choice. Whatever you choose, God, I choose You.

The conclusion of the matter:

God told me, "When everything is wrong, I'm right—right here for you! You are mine, and that which is mine is important to me." I am now living in my Canaan land. God has delivered me! My forty-year dispensation is over! I am complete in Him!

God, I love You with my whole heart, mind, and spirit.

"Count it all joy!" (James 1:2). Philosophy may instruct men to be calm in understanding their troubles,; but God teaches His children to be joyful.

The Power of Joy

Rejoice in the Lord always, and again I say rejoice! This is the power of joy! Our God! Our sustainable source!

> But now thus saith the LORD that created thee, O Jacob, and he that formed thee, O Israel, Fear not: for I have redeemed thee, I have called *thee* by thy name; thou *art* mine. When thou passest through the waters, I *will be* with thee; and through the rivers, they shall not overflow thee: when thou walkest through the fire, thou shalt not be burned; neither shall the flame kindle upon thee. For I *am* the LORD thy God, the Holy One of Israel, thy Saviour. (Isaiah 43:1–3)

> The Blessing of the Lord maketh rich and added no sorrow to it. (Proverbs 10:22)

I made up my mind that I would not be sorrowful. I would be rich in praise, rich in joy, rich in faith, and rich in patience. Then I realized that the people around me were not adding to the richness God wanted me to have, so I declared, "No more of your doom and gloom! You are blocking my light. Step away from the building." God is good. Now I can bask in His glorious light, minus dark clouds.

Your Thoughts